For Deltaloy, 8/2

Today is "someday"!

Peace & Light

David Dawson

A Reminder to My Twenty-Three-Year Old Self

A Book of Quotes, Thoughts on Life, and Personal Wisdom

DAVID DAMIAN FIGUEROA

Copyright © 2019 David Damian Figueroa.

All rights reserved. No part of this book may be reproduced, stored, or transmitted by any means—whether auditory, graphic, mechanical, or electronic—without written permission of the author, except in the case of brief excerpts used in critical articles and reviews. Unauthorized reproduction of any part of this work is illegal and is punishable by law.

ISBN: 978-1-6847-0244-2 (sc)
ISBN: 978-1-6847-0246-6 (hc)
ISBN: 978-1-6847-0245-9 (e)

Library of Congress Control Number: 2019904539

Because of the dynamic nature of the Internet, any web addresses or links contained in this book may have changed since publication and may no longer be valid. The views expressed in this work are solely those of the author and do not necessarily reflect the views of the publisher, and the publisher hereby disclaims any responsibility for them.

Any people depicted in stock imagery provided by Getty Images are models, and such images are being used for illustrative purposes only.
Certain stock imagery © Getty Images.

Lulu Publishing Services rev. date: 04/17/2019

For my mother,

Antonia Hernandez Figueroa

Introduction

When I was a young boy, my mother repeated *dichos*, Mexican folk sayings, and American quotes as part of everyday life. My mother had been a child farmworker and only reached the sixth grade. What she might have lacked in a formal education, she made up for with powerful words of wisdom. Dichos were her way of teaching me to become a better person.

As a single mother, she knew how to carve out a living. She worked as a field worker, maid, seamstress, cook, caregiver, school bus driver, and more. She rarely had money to pay a babysitter, so I accompanied her to her various jobs. My earliest memories are of being out in the agricultural fields of Buckeye, Arizona, with her, my aunts, and my cousins. Hardship was a part of life, but Mom would always say something positive to keep us going—something as simple and promising as "Life is not always going to be like this" or "This is only temporary, and *todo es possible*" (Anything is possible).

My mother taught me to have faith, pray, sew, cook, clean house, wash clothes, iron, change a tire, run a lawn mower, and even do arts and crafts. She'd tell me, "You have to learn how to do all of these things because one day I will not be here." She was right. Mom passed away tragically when she was only forty-eight years old. When parents pass away, the loudest voices we hear are theirs. The dicho that has stood out most in my life is "Con dinero se puede comprar libros pero no la educación" (You can purchase books with money, but money will not buy you an education or proper manners).

I was twenty-three when my mother passed away. For several years, life seemed almost impossible to navigate as I stumbled through day by day, making plenty of mistakes along the way.

Now in my fifties, almost a decade older than my mother was when she died, I reflect on my life and my decisions and contemplate what I would have done differently if given a chance to do it all over. At one point, I concluded that I would have become a different person, but I didn't like that idea much, for despite the obstacles I faced (most by my own doing), I created a solid body of work that spans more than three decades. My accomplishments were fueled by the praise I continually received for a job well done, but after the high from the praise subsided, I was left with a feeling of emptiness and an overwhelming sense of inadequacy.

Through the decades, I developed a pattern of jotting down quick thoughts and making mental notes about my experiences. I found I'd inherited my mother's love of quotes, and those, like my vivid memories of her, helped me to heal through tough times. In each quote I write, I always hear my mother's voice.

In 2012, the UCLA Chicano Studies Research Center (CSRC) invited me to donate my archive, a life's work in philanthropy, arts, entertainment, and activism. A few years later, I helped curate an exhibition of my archive. Seeing my professional life laid out before me, I could not help but think of my mother and all she taught me. To honor her and my body of work, I paired her sayings—dichos—with items in my life that were most meaningful. That was how I came up with the idea of someday writing this book.

Throughout the years, I have come up with my own original quotes, thoughts on life, and personal wisdom, which have helped to keep me from repeating mistakes. These have come to me in moments when I've felt I wanted to reconcile the past, process the present, and be optimistic about the future. My favorites have made their way into this book.

My mother will live forever with me through the love and wisdom she gave to me through her dichos. They have left an indelible impression in my mind, and I am her grateful son.

Today I open my heart, eyes, mind, and soul.

I'm ready to receive all that is good.

A dream is achieved with vision, faith, and one decisive action at a time.

Today I will create an action plan for my dream.

What we see is limited to what we can imagine.

Today I will imagine a life of happiness and fulfillment.

Honoring a person's point of view, respecting his or her beliefs, acknowledging hard work, and recognizing our own mistakes are acts of love.

Today I will be loving.

If you don't set your own value, someone will set it for you.

I am invaluable.

The most threatening thing to an unhappy person is a happy person.

Today I choose happiness.

There's no need to pack your emotional baggage when traveling to the future.

Today I will work toward unloading emotional baggage.

Surviving through life is merely existing while putting off our growth and spiritual evolution.

Today I will make a list of things that
enhance my personal evolution.

Forgiveness is not a comfortable act. It asks us to transform ourselves from a state of ego to a state of peace.

Am I at peace? Who do I need to forgive?

A harsh critic is merely a person who judges others from a throne of ego while masking fear that his or her own mediocre talent will be exposed.

Am I happy for others? Do I criticize others?

There is no greater wealth than the gift of experiencing life each day or the time we have left.

What will I do to make the most of each day?

If you are at a standstill in assessing an important decision, ask yourself whether the direction you choose will serve a higher purpose or your ego.

What is the purpose of the direction I am taking in my life?

Our inaction can also be an action. Staying silent when we should have said something, doing nothing when our participation might have made a difference, and not helping when we could have helped are all action items.

Do I speak up when I or others experience an injustice?

There's nothing more valuable than peace.

What will I do to ensure I am at peace?

No one holds the key to your success. Only you can decide who and what you will be.

What is my definition of success? What kind of person will I be when I am successful?

Now that you have everyone's attention, what is your responsibility? What is your message? What kind of person will you be?

What kind of message do I want to impart on others?

Your past is behind you. Now walk away.

Is my past keeping me from moving forward?

Who you were and what you did are not as important as who you are now and what you've yet to become.

Who am I? What kind of person do I want to be?

Faith is a knowing that all things are possible.

Am I hopeful or fearful about my future?

My faith in humanity is unshakable.

Do I try to see the good in people?

Be quiet. Be still. Be peaceful. Be sure that the answer lies within.

What will I do to quiet my mind?

Things that enlighten our minds, nourish our bodies, and breathe new life into our souls are all worthy of doing.

What do I do daily to nourish my mind, body, and soul?

My age is none of my business, and it shouldn't be yours either.

Am I insecure about growing older?

I believe that God created women as His most loving gift to the world. He knew they would be peacemakers and make enormous contributions and sacrifices that would benefit His children. He knew that women would lead the world with compassion, wisdom, peace, truth, and love.

What will I do to honor women?

Spending time with a great friend feels like breathing in blessings. Friends listen to us in good times and in our hours of despair. They allow us to be vulnerable, and they embrace us with their authentic selves.

Do I feel safe when telling my true feelings when I'm with my closest friends?

There is an abundance of light. Sharing some of yours with a friend will not diminish it from continuing to shine on you.

Do I share my success with others?

Our pursuit of wisdom and enlightenment will greatly reduce our suffering.

What will I do to continually evolve as a person?
What am I willing to do to secure my happiness?

Meditation and prayer each morning will lead to clarity, peace, love, optimism, and happiness.

What daily practices do I implement that help to secure my happiness?

Once you reach the mountaintop, there's only one thing that will cause you to tumble: your ego.

What will I do daily to keep my ego in check?

Feelings of fear, anger, and resentment are opposite of peace, love, and joy. Be careful which ones you choose. One will prevent you from feeling the other.

Do I feel that I am in control of choosing peace, love, and joy?

It's not kind to call someone a has-been. I believe it's better to have been than never to have been.

How do I honor the accomplishments of others?

Unresolved anger serves as a huge disservice to our souls and is the highest expression of the ego mind.

Is my anger really a need to forgive myself or someone else?

Anger obstructs all blessings. It can be eliminated only through acts of kindness, love, and compassion toward the subject of our anger.

What are some of the things I do to keep blessings from entering my life?

In times of uncertainty, try not to lose sense of the time you have right now.

Do I increase my anxiety by mindless catastrophic thinking?

Anxiety is a clear indication that what we are doing consciously is not working for us. The ego mind fools us into believing that it can heal what prayer and meditation cannot.

What will I do daily to break old habits
and rethink long-held ideals?

Choose people, places, and things carefully.

What are my criteria for choosing people, places, and things that enter my life? What do I need to change?

Negativity slows down our personal evolution and obstructs all miracles from entering our lives.

What do I do to keep my thoughts and environment positive?

**Life is not always about winning.
It's about not losing your character
while trying to get to the finish line.**

What do I learn when I lose?

**Prayer alone is not enough. Action is also required….
and faith that our actions will make
manifest what we pray for.**

What actions will I take today to secure my hopes and dreams?

We can buy the best education or reach the upper echelons of society, but good manners are not for sale, and they must accompany us wherever we go.

My thoughts.

It is important to recognize when emotional chaos is coming down the road. We can easily take a detour, but there are also valuable lessons to be learned in driving right through it with compassion, grace, and dignity.

What can I do to prevent emotional chaos?

At the end of the day, we can reflect on what we can achieve tomorrow that will help us to be better versions of ourselves.

Do I spend time in reflection before the start of a new day?

People who think a person is too old to do something they believe only a young person should do have antiquated thinking.

Do I ever judge others unfairly because of their age?

Miracles do happen. To experience them in our lives, with full abundance, we must eliminate negativity in all forms.

What will I do to eliminate negativity in my life?

If each person on earth were to demonstrate, just for one day, the supreme virtues of love, faith, hope, charity, mercy, and forgiveness, just think how we could collectively transform the world we live in.

Today is someday.

Never underestimate the possibility of a miracle.

Life is like a game of chess: we must constantly figure out our next best and most strategic move.

Each person has the inherent ability to decide what is needed in his or her life to be happy.

Do not let your dreams go by the wayside as you move through life. Before you know it, decades pass, fear sets in, and dreams dissolve.

What is the definition of *success*? For some, it could mean just having peace.

Success doesn't happen by chance; it happens when we work with divine purpose and determination and honor the people we engage with.

Within each of us exists a deep well of divine inspiration. It can only be tapped when we act with purposeful intention. The well only runs dry when we are negative or surrounded by negativity.

Time spent believing that all things are possible is time well spent.

Positive energy in our daily lives is like water that flows with ease and grace.

It takes courage to proclaim your hopes, dreams, and ideas.

He or she who brings peace and respect to every situation holds the power.

Prayer and meditation are the keys to opening the doors to a universe filled with blessings.

If I get it wrong repeatedly, I need to keep trying until I get it right. Life will continue to repeat an unwanted experience until I have learned the lesson necessary for a permanent breakthrough.

Haters are not your worst enemies; your ego is.

Everyone deserves to be appreciated. One of the most meaningful acts of kindness is to express our appreciation toward others. Appreciation demonstrates that a good deed did not go unnoticed, nor was it taken for granted.

Each day, hour, minute, and second, we have an opportunity to go back to center. Sundays are God's gift and a reminder for us to recalibrate our spirits.

If you are the most intelligent person on the planet, then you need to explore the universe.

Your personal support system should consist of happy people or those in serious pursuit of happiness.

Our single most important role on earth is to be of service to others. Service gives us purpose and brings meaning to our lives.

Always be the silver lining in every situation.

**Sometimes saying nothing is saying a lot.
Sometimes doing nothing is enough.**

Our thoughts of fear have no real value. Turn them into thoughts that do have value.

The best cure for boredom is service to others. There's nothing boring about making a difference in someone else's life.

You see a person's true character when he or she no longer needs you for access.

It's inevitable that the universe will cause change to occur in our lives. It's easier on our spirits if we initiate and embrace change rather than being forced to accept change.

Our best ideas will only get us to a certain point unless they are guided by a higher principle.

Forgetting where you came from is dishonoring who you are.

The ability to see people for who they really are, and not what we would like them to be, is a gift.

The past is done. All we have is today. Today is a gift and an opportunity to create the lives we always knew we could have.

Never rule out someone with a big dream. You never know if you will need him or her to help make yours happen.

If one person wins and everybody else loses, there are no winners.

The greatest shows on earth are the sun rising and the moon appearing. They do that every day; we just don't notice.

Hate is a disease that is curable.

I grant myself permission to feel what I feel.

Someone who is silent is either a good listener or trying to control you.

Be yourself no matter what. Being yourself will allow you to live among the free.

You have a problem?
What are you going to do about it?
Don't blame anyone.

Forgiveness is freedom.

Don't interrupt others when they're talking, and don't allow anyone to interrupt you when you're talking.

Keep your head up, smile, and act like you're going somewhere. Eventually, you will get there.

People-pleasing will lead to your displeasure.

Volunteer whenever you can. It will give you something interesting to talk about, and it will build your character.

Be generous.
Be kind.
Be compassionate.
Be empathetic.
Be loving.
Life will be easier.

The words *no* and *yes* will change your life dramatically. Choose carefully.

If you are always doing all the listening, that means the other person is not interested in anything about you.

Love transforms and heals all living things.

God does exist.

After our parents pass away, the loudest voices we hear are theirs.

The last words spoken to anyone should be kind words.

Good manners will keep doors open.

Always take something when you go to visit someone, even if it's just your gratitude.

Always treat anyone who is serving you with kindness, generosity, and respect.

Designer clothes do not make you important.

If you say you're not good enough, people will believe you.

If you tell someone not to share your secret, odds are that he or she will.

The same person will continue to reappear throughout your life, only with a different face, unless you stop attracting him or her.

People don't change; they just cover up who they are temporarily.

**You're going to be okay.
You're going to get through this.
It's going to take work.
The outcome is up to you.**

Be careful how much and to whom you give. Not everyone is deserving of your generosity.

Not everyone will like you, and that's okay.

If someone intentionally ignores you to make you feel invisible, make sure that person never gets to see you again.

Sometimes we don't get to see justice or karma take form, but that doesn't mean they were not served up.

Complaining leads to nothing, but action will lead you to everything.

When you love someone with all your heart and being, be sure he or she loves you in the same way.

The feelings of betrayal subside with time.

Choose your words carefully. Words can cause irreparable damage or create paradise.

Accept yourself for who you are, who you were, and who you've yet to become.

You don't need anyone's approval. The only approval you need is God's approval. He accepts you no matter what.

Make yourself a priority in your own life.

People don't change; they only adjust their behavior for situations that benefit their needs.

When we speak from the ego, we forget who we are.

Never try to justify yourself to someone who has already tried and convicted you with no evidence.